GHOSTS & MONSTERS

by **Jason Page**

Contents

Cle

Copyright © 2006 **ticktock** Entertainment Ltd.

http://www.ticktock.co.uk

GREECE IS THE WORD

Some of the oldest and scariest stories came from the ancient Greeks. These myths and legends were first told more than 4,500 years ago, and describe some truly nasty creatures. Fortunately, there was usually a brave hero around to save the day.

DOWN, BOY!

The Greeks believed that when someone died their spirit went to a place called Hades. The entrance to Hades was guarded by a fearsome dog named Cerberus. He had three heads, each with a mouth full of terrible teeth, and his tail was made of snakes. Cerberus' job was to stop dead spirits leaving Hades and prevent those who had not died from entering.

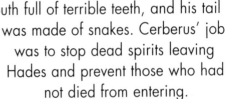

FACT OR FICTION?

King Minos really did exist. During the 1970s, archaeologists discovered the remains of his palace and a sprawling maze of secret tunnels. Could this have been the legendary Labyrinth?

C-EYE-CLOPS

The Cyclops were a race of cruel, ugly giants. They were also easy to recognise because they had only one eye – in the middle of their forehead! In one famous story, a Cyclops called Polyphemus captured a Greek ship and ate six of the crew for dinner.

2

HAIR SSSSTYLE

Medusa was a truly terrifying Gorgon. Instead of hair, her head was covered by a mass of writhing snakes. She had the power to turn people into stone just by looking at them. Fortunately, a young hero called Perseus managed to defeat her. He used his shield to show Medusa her own reflection. Not surprisingly, she turned to stone – and Perseus chopped off her head!

MONSTER IN A MAZE

According to legend, the palace of King Minos in Crete was also home to a terrible monster. It was known as the Minotaur and was half-human and half-bull. It lived in an endless maze of tunnels called the Labyrinth. Every year, seven young boys and seven young girls from Athens were led into the Labyrinth... never to be seen again!

MONSTER QUIZ

How did the remaining Greek crew members escape from Polyphemus?

a) they pushed a wooden spike into his eye while he was asleep
b) they poisoned him
c) they pushed him over a cliff

How did Theseus manage not to get lost in the Minotaur's Labyrinth?

a) he used a map and compass
b) he unravelled some wool, leaving a trail behind him
c) he had a guide with him

What could the blood from the right side of Medusa's body do?

a) it could revive the dead
b) it could make people invisible
c) it could turn things into gold

(answers on page 32)

MONSTER QUIZ

What did Frankenstein do that really upset his monster?

a) sewed his ears on upside down
b) refused to make him a girlfriend
c) called him 'Ugly-mug'

Which of these books was written by Robert Louis Stevenson?

a) *Robinson Crusoe*
b) *20,000 Leagues Under the Sea*
c) *Treasure Island*

Which of these statements about William Brody is true?

a) he stole the Scottish Crown Jewels
b) he was a very honest man
c) he had built the gallows on which he was executed

(answers on page 32)

NOVEL BEGINNINGS

The famous story of *Frankenstein* was written by Mary Shelley in 1818. It is about a doctor who creates a monster using parts from dead bodies. He then brings it to life using electricity. At first, the monster is quite friendly. Unfortunately, everyone treats it cruelly because they are afraid of it – and this makes the monster mad!

MISERABLE MONSTER

In the original story, the monster kills Dr Frankenstein and his family before escaping to the Arctic. Most of the films made about Frankenstein's monster ignore the moral of Shelley's tale – which is that if everyone had treated the monster well in the first place, it would never have turned into such a brute.

REAL-LIFE HYDE

The book *Dr Jekyll and Mr Hyde* was inspired by the real-life story of William Brody. Brody was a master carpenter who lived in Edinburgh, Scotland. By day, he pretended to be a highly respectable person, but at night he used to break into people's houses and do all sorts of terrible things. He was finally caught and hanged in 1788.

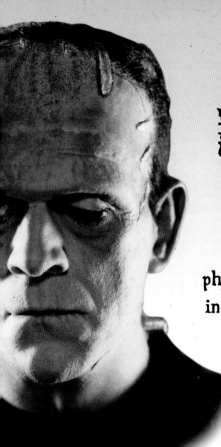

MAD DOCTORS

No one would want to be one of Dr Frankenstein's patients - nor Dr Jekyll's. These two freaky physicians had some nasty skeletons in the cupboard, but luckily, they are only story book characters.

WHAT'S IN A NAME

?

SPLIT PERSONALITY

The character of Dr Jekyll was created by Robert Louis Stevenson for his book *Dr Jekyll and Mr Hyde* (1886). However, Dr Jekyll isn't really one character but two! In Stevenson's story, the 'good' Dr Jekyll drinks a potion which turns him into the wicked Mr Hyde. As Mr Hyde, he commits all sorts of hideous crimes but when the effects of the potion wear off, he turns back into Dr Jekyll and is horrified at what he has done.

Most people think that Frankenstein is the name of the monster. It isn't! Frankenstein was the doctor who created the monster. The monster was never given a name.

SEEING IS BELIEVING

You may not believe in monsters, but many people claim to have seen them. Some even say they've got photos to prove it. So if monsters exist, where do they live?

DISTANT RELATIVES?

There are many eyewitness reports from all around the world of monsters that live high in the mountains. These creatures are said to look like giant apes. One theory is that they are our ancient ancestors. They seem to be very shy and often the only evidence of them is huge footprints in the snow.

SAY 'CHEESE'

Loch Ness is a vast, deep lake in Scotland, said to be the home of the most famous monster of them all. The first reported sighting of the Loch Ness monster was more than 1,400 years ago. Since then, hundreds of people claim to have seen it. This photograph of 'Nessie' was taken in 1983.

MONSTER MOVIE

The most famous encounter with a mountain monster occurred in 1967 in Northern California, USA. A man named Roger Patterson was riding his horse when a large, hairy, ape-like creature walked out of the trees in front of him. Patterson's horse reared up and threw him off, but he was able to grab his cine camera and film the monster before it returned to the woods.

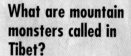

MONSTER QUIZ

What are mountain monsters called in Tibet?
a) beti
b) yeti
c) heti

What are mountain monsters called in Russia?
a) Alama
b) Elma
c) Anna

Some people think that the Loch Ness monster is a type of plesiosaur – what is this?
a) a member of the dolphin family
b) a prehistoric creature that lived in water
c) a giant eel

(answers on page 32)

Monster footprints found at the side of Loch Ness in the 1930s turned out to have been made using the foot of a stuffed hippopotamus!

NESSIE ISN'T ALONE

Loch Ness isn't the only lake with a monster. Lake Nahooin in Ireland and Bear Lake in Utah, USA, both have their own monster residents. Another legendary creature is the Ogopgo, said to live in Lake Okenagen in British Columbia.

GEORGE: 1, DRAGON: 0

The most famous dragon-slayer is probably St. George. According to one famous legend this brave knight rescued a beautiful princess from a wicked dragon, killing the monster with his lance. But not all heroes are so successful. An Old English poem tells the story of another adventurer, named Beowulf, who lost his life trying to steal a dragon's treasure.

TREASURE TRAIL

In European stories, dragons are almost always evil, scaly monsters. Often they can breathe fire, and have wings and a pointed tail just like a demon. Such dragons usually live in a cave or lair that's full of treasure. Anyone brave enough to steal the treasure must slay the dragon first!

FEROCIOUS DRAGONS

On some islands in Indonesia, dragons are all too frighteningly real! These islands are home to giant lizards known as Komodo dragons. Growing to more than 3 metres long, these monster reptiles have razor-sharp claws and saw-like teeth. They are ferocious hunters, capable of killing goats, wild pigs and even people.

HERE BE DRAGONS

Terrifying lizard-monsters or symbols of good luck? Different people have very different ideas about dragons. It all depends on where you come from...

FRIENDLY DRAGONS

In China, dragons are treated with great respect and are thought to bring good luck. To celebrate the Chinese New Year, groups of people parade through the streets wearing big dragon costumes. According to ancient tradition, this stops evil spirits spoiling the new year.

MONSTER DRAGON

A Komodo dragon can weigh up to 160 kg – that's as heavy as five ten-year-old children!

BLOODSUCKERS

Legend tells of vampire corpses who rise nightly from the grave. As you are about to discover, these bloodthirsty ghouls can be a real pain in the neck – and so can real-life vampire bats!

MAKING A KILLING

It's not easy to destroy a vampire; the most reliable way is to expose it to sunlight, shoot it with a silver bullet or drive a wooden stake through its heart. If you want to check whether someone really is a vampire, just hold a mirror up to their face – vampires have no reflection!

FACT OR FICTION?

The story of Count Dracula, the most famous vampire of all time, was written by Bram Stoker in 1897. But what's really scary is that *Dracula* is based on a real person! During the 1400s, part of Transylvania was ruled by Vlad Tepes, also known as Count Dracul. The bloodthirsty Count liked to kill his enemies by driving a wooden stake through their bodies and, according to local people, he also drank their blood!

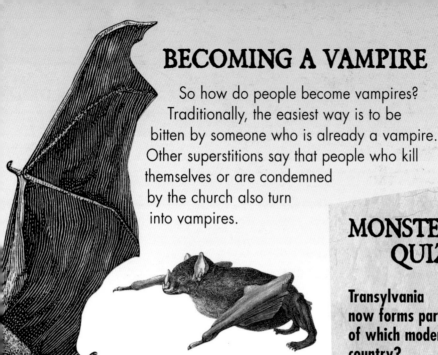

BECOMING A VAMPIRE

So how do people become vampires? Traditionally, the easiest way is to be bitten by someone who is already a vampire. Other superstitions say that people who kill themselves or are condemned by the church also turn into vampires.

COMPLETELY BATTY

In many horror stories, vampires are able to change themselves into bats. And vampire bats really do exist! They feed by biting a small hole in the neck of another animal then lapping up the blood with their tongues.

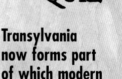

MONSTER QUIZ

Transylvania now forms part of which modern country?
a) Bulgaria
b) Romania
c) Portugal

Which of these things wouldn't scare off a vampire?
a) garlic
b) crosses
c) mice

Where are you most likely to find a vampire bat?
a) Central and South America
b) Asia and Africa
c) Transylvania

(answers on page 32)

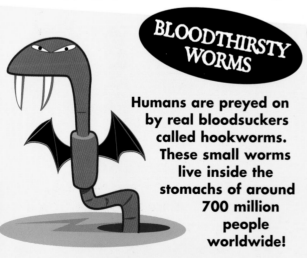

BLOODTHIRSTY WORMS

Humans are preyed on by real bloodsuckers called hookworms. These small worms live inside the stomachs of around 700 million people worldwide!

MONSTER QUIZ

A werewolf known as the Beast of Gévaudan caused terror in France between 1764 and 1767. How many people are supposed to have been killed?

a) 16
b) 40
c) 75 or more

Which of these is another name for a werewolf?

a) lycanthrope
b) Wolf Spirit
c) snapping he-devil

The last wolf in Britain is supposed to have been killed in which year?

a) 1201
b) 1452
c) 1680

(answers on page 32)

REAL WOLF-PEOPLE?

No, the people in this picture aren't wearing make-up! They had a very rare genetic condition called congenital generalised hypertrichosis (CGH for short), also known as werewolf syndrome. It causes thick hair to grow all over their bodies, including their faces, making them look just like real-life werewolves.

ALL CHANGE

Werewolves are supposed to be able to change from a human into a wolf. How they do this varies from story to story, but methods include drinking the rainwater that collects in a wolf's footprint, looking at a full moon or putting on a wolf's skin.

THE REAL KILLERS

Scary stories of werewolves probably came about because people in Europe have always been afraid of wolves – even though wolves very rarely attack people! This fear also led to wolf packs being ruthlessly hunted down and killed, so that today they survive in only a handful of places.

WOLFMEN!

Part-human, part-wolf, werewolves are strong, cunning and hungry for human flesh. Stories of these terrible creatures may date back to long ago, but they can still send a chill down our spines today.

STRANGE BUT TRUE

One of the best werewolf sightings is said to have occurred at Bungay Church in Suffolk. According to local legend, in 1577 a ferocious werewolf attacked members of the congregation, killing two and leaving another with terrible burns. It then ran off to nearby Blythburgh Church and clawed at the door, trying to get inside. That was the last anyone saw of the monster, but the deep claw marks on the church door can still be seen to this day!

FOOD FOR THOUGHT

Real wolves have a huge appetite. An adult wolf can eat 9 kg of food at a time – that's the same as 80 hamburgers!

PICTURE THIS

The devil is top of the list when it comes to evil spirits. The Bible depicts him as a fiendish tempter who revels in human wrongdoings. Many artists have tried to emphasise the devil's evil nature by painting him in red, the colour of anger and temptation.

TERRIBLE TEETH

Tasmanian devils really live up to their name. They have ferocious fangs and, when threatened, will attack almost anything, including people!

STRANGE BUT TRUE

On 8 February 1895, people living in five different towns in Devon, woke up to a chilling sight. During the night it had snowed, but it wasn't the cold weather that made their hair stand on end. Everywhere they looked there were cloven footprints – in their gardens, on the road, even on people's roofs. It seemed as though the devil had walked all over Devon!

DASTARDLY DEVILS

Devils and demons are bad — and proud of it! They like doing anything that's wrong, but what really makes some of them happy is tempting humans to do wrong, too.

EASTERN DEMONS

In many oriental religions there isn't just one devil, but lots, in all shapes and sizes! Almost all of them are extremely ugly, but some are more wicked that others. In fact, several of these eastern demons aren't really evil at all – they are just mischievous and like playing tricks on people.

REAL DEVIL

The Tasmanian devil may look quite cute, but it's a real devil. About the same size as a badger, it lives on the island of Tasmania, off the southern coast of Australia. It is a nocturnal creature that spends most of the day asleep and comes out at night to hunt small animals.

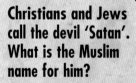

MONSTER QUIZ

Christians and Jews call the devil 'Satan'. What is the Muslim name for him?

a) Isis
b) Issab
c) Iblis

What sort of animal is a Tasmanian devil?

a) a reptile
b) a marsupial
c) an amphibian

Which of these is another name for the devil?

a) Lewis
b) Lucinda
c) Lucifer

(answers on page 32)

MONSTER QUIZ

According to
Dr Taha, what
caused the 'curse'?

a) a deadly bacteria
   sealed in the tomb
b) poisonous dust
   scattered near
   the entrance
c) malaria spread
   by mosquitoes

How old was
Tutankhamen
when he died?

a) 18
b) 56
c) 104

What's inside an
Egyptian mummy?

a) a statue made of gold
b) straw
c) a dried-out dead body

(answers on page 32)

CURSED CANARY

Howard Carter had a pet canary. Local workers believed the bird had guided them to the site of the burial chamber. However, a few weeks after the discovery of the tomb, the canary met a grisly end. It was eaten by a king cobra! In Egyptian times this deadly snake was often used to symbolise Tutankhamen!

AN UNSOLVED MYSTERY

The curse claimed further victims: George Bendit an archaeologist, and Arthur Mace, one of Carter's friends. Both men visited the tomb – and both died shortly afterwards. Carter remained untouched by the curse, but it didn't go away. In 1962, a scientist named Dr Ezzedin Taha claimed to have discovered the cause of the curse, but he died a few days later in a car crash.

BITE OF DEATH

Another victim was Lord Caernarvon, who had paid for Carter's expedition. He suddenly fell ill after an insect bite became mysteriously infected. A few weeks later, he was dead. He was only 53! At the very moment he was pronounced dead, all the lights in Cairo suddenly went out.

16

CURSE OF THE PHARAOHS

The ancient Egyptians placed a terrible curse on anyone who dared to disturb the magnificent graves of their kings. Thousands of years later, it seems that the power of this mysterious curse could be at work...

DISCOVERY!

On 26 November 1922, Howard Carter, an English archaeologist, discovered the tomb of an ancient king named Tutankhamen in the Egyptian desert. The pharaoh's burial chamber had remained undisturbed for 32 centuries. Carter was delighted. Tutankhamen, it seems, wasn't so pleased!

I WANT MY MUMMY

The ancient Egyptians didn't just make mummies of their ancestors. They also mummified their pet cats!

SPELLBOUND

Hubble bubble, toil and trouble...There are many stories about wicked witches cackling over their cauldrons and casting evil spells. But who were the real monsters — the witches or the witch-hunters?

MONSTER QUIZ

The revolting ingredients for the Brew-ha-ha spell above appear in a play by which famous writer?

a) Enid Blyton
b) Charles Dickens
c) William Shakespeare

What is a group of witches called?

a) a cover
b) a coven
c) an oven

Which of these is another word for a witch's spell?

a) a hex
b) a hoax
c) a vex

(answers on page 32)

SHAPE-SHIFTERS

Witches are said to have many magic powers. These include the ability to change shape or turn themselves into animals; fly (using a tool such as a rake or broom); cast spells and make magic potions.

WITCH ATTACK

From the late 1500s to the early 1700s, a huge witch-hunt took place in Europe and North America. Thousands of people (mostly women and girls) were falsely accused of being witches and put on trial. Suspected witches were thrown into rivers, stabbed with long needles and crushed under heavy stones. If they were found guilty of witchcraft, they were usually burned at the stake.

Here's a well-known recipe for making a spell: eye of newt, toe of frog, wool of bat and tongue of dog, lots of poisoned entrails, a toad and some fillet of snake. Hmmm, delicious...!

DASTARDLY DOLLS

Never give a wicked witch a bit of your hair – or even an old toenail clipping! She'll use it to make a doll called a fetish. Then, whatever the witch does to the doll is supposed to happen to you, too. By putting pins in the doll she can cause pain in different parts of your body. Ouch!

WHICH WITCH?

Witchcraft isn't just a thing of the past. There are many people who call themselves witches today. Modern witchcraft, often called Wicca, is like a religion or faith. These modern witches are a far cry from the evil witches in stories like the one shown here. They try to use magic to create good, for example, by curing people who are ill.

FRIGHTNIGHT

Hallowe'en is the scariest night of the year. So when 31 October comes round, who knows what ghosts and ghouls may come knocking at your door!

MEAN JACK

People often make lanterns for Hallowe'en by carving faces in hollow pumpkins. These are called Jack o' lanterns after an old Irish miser called Jack. The story goes that Jack was so mean with his money, God wouldn't let him into Heaven, but the Devil wouldn't let him into Hell either. So, Jack was forced to wander the Earth carrying his lantern until Judgement Day.

SPOOKS' NIGHT

Hallowe'en has been a special spooky night for more than 2,000 years. An ancient people called the Celts believed that this was the one night of the year when Samhain, the god of death, allowed the souls of dead people to roam the Earth and return to their old homes.

SAINTLY BEGINNINGS?

Hallowe'en is so-called because it is the evening before the Christian festival of All Hallows Day – an old English name for All Saints' Day. On this day, poor people used to go 'a-souling' – this meant they begged for money and promised to pray for anyone who gave them some. The modern 'trick-or-treat' game probably comes from this tradition.

REVEALING PEEL

Lots of Hallowe'en superstitions are to do with fortune-telling. For instance, if a girl peels off an entire apple skin without breaking it, then throws it over her shoulder at midnight on Hallowe'en, the shape the skin makes when it lands is supposed to reveal the first letter of her future husband's name!

APPLE-Y EVER AFTER

Of course, not all superstitions are true!

MONSTER QUIZ

In Scotland, children make a 'Hallowe'en bleeze' to celebrate Hallowe'en – what is this?

a) a big fruit cake
b) a big, scary mask
c) a big bonfire to scare away evil spirits

What or who was Feralia?

a) a Roman festival held on Hallowe'en in honour of the dead
b) the Viking god of death and destruction
c) a Roman village that completely disappeared on Hallowe'en in 1731

Which of these is another name for Hallowe'en?

a) Snap Apple Night
b) Crack Bone Night
c) Pop Shiver Night

(answers on page 32)

MONSTER QUIZ

Which of these is the name of a famous Hollywood horror movie star?

a) Stella Lutosi
b) Bela Lugosi
c) Jelly Ambrosia

What is the name of the character played by Christina Ricci in *The Addams Family*?

a) Monday
b) Tuesday
c) Wednesday

What was Boris Karloff's real name?

a) William Henry Pratt
b) Peter Pickleswick III
c) Valentine Ignatus Bumblesbloomer

(answers on page 32)

IT'S A SCREAM!

When a horror film called *The Exorcist* was shown at the Alla Park Cinema in Australia, the entire audience were frightened out of their wits – but not because of the scary film. It was the spooky goings-on inside the cinema that terrified the audience. Strange noises were heard and light bulbs blew all over the building. Some of the audience were so scared they left – before the film had even started!

SPOOKY ACTRESS

Christina Ricci starred in her first film about spooks, *The Addams Family*, when she was only 11 years old. She went on to appear in two more ghostly films, *Addams Family Values* and *Casper the Friendly Ghost* (above

MONSTER MOVIES

Ghosts, ghouls and monsters are big business in Hollywood. The first horror movies were made back in the 1920s, and today scary films are as popular as ever.

HORROR HERO

Dracula has been portrayed in more films than any other character apart from Sherlock Holmes.

SCARY ACTOR

The actor Boris Karloff was famous for playing spooky roles and starred in more than a hundred horror films. He shot to fame as Frankenstein's monster in a film made in 1931, and was still scaring the life out of movie-goers more than 30 years later.

SPOOKY SIGHTINGS

Do ghosts really exist? No one knows for sure, but quite a few people claim to have seen one, and there are stories of hauntings in many different parts of the world.

GHOSTS WITH PLUCK

The most haunted village in the world is said to be Pluckley in Kent. It has no less than 14 resident spooks – including a screaming man, a mysterious red lady and a monk.

SPOOKY SNAPSHOT

In the summer of 1988, tourist Lars Thomas visited London, England, and went on a guided tour of The Viaduct Inn. The cellars at this inn used to be Newgate Prison and are said to be haunted by a ghost or poltergeist. Fascinated, Lars Thomas decided to take a photo of a cell, and waited until he was sure that no one was in front of him. However, when the photo was developed, a mysterious figure appeared in the picture (left).

A HAUNTING TAIL

Not all ghosts are human. The ghost of a small dog has been seen quite regularly on a beach in Dorset. The dog is believed to have belonged to a Chinese princess who sailed from China to visit Queen Elizabeth I more than 400 years ago. The poor pet was killed when the ship's crew threw it overboard into the sea – along with the princess! Their bodies were washed up on the beach and it seems their ghosts have stayed there ever since.

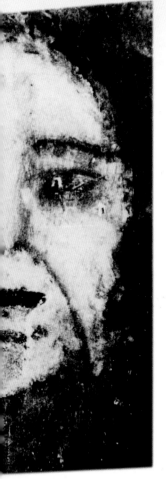

FLOORED BY FACES

In 1971, a Spanish woman named Maria Gomez Pereira noticed a strange mark on her kitchen floor. It looked like a face. She tried to clean it off but the mark wouldn't budge. Her son even replaced part of the floor but it did no good – the face just came back. Soon other faces started appearing (left). Investigations revealed that the house had been built on the site of an ancient cemetery. New faces continue to appear on the floor to this day, although scientists can't explain why!

MONSTER QUIZ

Whose ghost has been seen the most times?

a) Anne Boleyn
b) Henry VIII
c) Jack the Ripper

In which of these books by Charles Dickens is there a ghost?

a) *A Christmas Carol*
b) *Oliver Twist*
c) *Bleak House*

The ghost of Wildenstein Castle in Germany has an annoying habit of...

a) falling down the stairs
b) appearing while people are having a bath
c) stealing visitors' luggage

(answers on page 32)

MONSTER QUIZ

How did *The Flying Dutchman* become a ghost ship?

a) the ship's crew were all killed by pirates

b) the ship was destroyed by a giant squid

c) the ship's captain made a bet with the devil and lost

Sailors who think they saw mermaids probably really saw a...

a) sea lion or sea cow

b) herring

c) lighthouse

How many mermaids did Christopher Columbus claim to have seen during his voyage to America in 1492?

a) 0

b) 3

c) 35

(answers on page 32)

ALL ABOARD?

In 1872, the crew of a British ship, the *Dei Gratia*, spotted another ship in the distance. As they approached, they noticed something very strange. Everything on board was in perfect order. There was just one thing missing: the crew! The ship, named the *Mary Celeste*, was completely deserted. No trace of the captain or his men were ever found.

SPOOKY SHIPS

Tales of ghost ships date back to Viking times. Hundreds of sailors claim to have seen one, including King George V. On 11 July 1881, Prince George (as he was at the time) was on *HMS Inconstant* when he claimed he saw the most famous ghost ship of them all – *The Flying Dutchman*!

A PLANE MYSTERY

It's not just old sailing ships that have ghostly crew members. The modern aircraft carrier *USS Forrestal*, belonging to the American Navy, is also said to be haunted. Several sailors have reported strange things happening on the ship – one even claimed that his leg was grabbed by the ghost as he climbed up a ladder!

ALL AT SEA

The stories of sea monsters and ghost ships are enough to send a shiver down anyone's timbers. Even the king of England was convinced the high seas were haunted!

MONSTERS OF THE DEEP

Sailors tell stories about life-or-death battles with terrifying sea creatures. These monsters of the deep include giant squid, octopuses and ferocious sharks. Although a giant squid has never been captured alive, these creatures really do exist. Dead specimens with tentacles more than 18 metres long have been found washed up along the shore.

SEA BEAUTIES

Sailors may have mistaken manatees or walruses for mermaids or other strange sea monsters.

POLTERGEISTS

Not content just to haunt people, poltergeists get up to all sorts of mischievous tricks. They don't just make things go bump in the night — they go smash, crash, bang, wallop too!

TEEN SPIRIT

UNDER ARREST!

In 1967, the police were called to arrest a poltergeist that was smashing cups and saucers in a china shop in Miami, USA.

Most ghost experts agree that poltergeists aren't caused by spirits of the dead, although films like *Poltergeist* (right) are based on this idea. Instead, poltergeists are thought to be created by the powerful psychic energy of living people – especially teenagers!

WAT-ER MYSTERY

One of the most famous cases of a poltergeist was recorded in 1977. Over a period of several months, a series of terrifying events occurred at the home of the Harper family in London. Pools of water appeared in the middle of rooms, heavy furniture and other objects were thrown around and several small fires broke out. There were many witnesses to these strange occurrences, although no one could explain them.

GHOSTBUSTER

The great ghost-hunter Harry Price was often called upon to investigate poltergeists. During the 1930s, Price even managed to film and photograph several of these spooks in action.

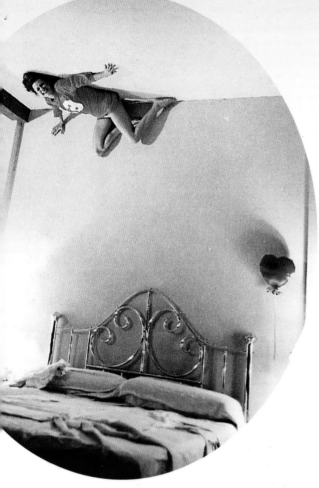

MONSTER QUIZ

Which famous writer helped to investigate a poltergeist in 1759?

a) William Shakespeare
b) Samuel Johnson
c) Roald Dahl

Reports of poltergeists date back to...

a) Roman times
b) AD 1000
c) the early 1500s

When investigating poltergeists, Harry Price always carried a small pot of mercury. What was it for?

a) protection against evil spirits
b) detecting slight vibrations or movements
c) working out the temperature

(answers on page 32)

WHAT'S IN A NAME?

The word 'poltergeist' is German. It means, literally, 'rattling ghost'. Poltergeists get their name because they tend to make such a lot of noise! However, although they cause a lot of damage, they very rarely hurt people.

PASS ON THE SALT

Want to get rid of a zombie? All you need is some salt. According to voodoo tradition, eating salt has the same effect on zombies as garlic does on vampires.

MONSTER QUIZ

What is another name for a voodoo sorcerer?

a) a witch doctor
b) a which doctor
c) a why doctor

Voodoo is a mixture of...

a) Christian and African beliefs
b) Muslim and Christian beliefs
c) Muslim and African beliefs

What name is given to a voodoo priest?

a) Houngan
b) Trasulmi
c) Ngana

(answers on page 32)

VOODOO GURUS

The way to turn someone into a zombie is to make them eat or drink a special poison made by a voodoo sorcerer. The zombie then becomes your slave. The only way to break the spell is to give the zombie some salt to eat.

BACK FROM THE DEAD

What do you get if you cross a ghost with a monster? The answer is...a zombie! Zombies are neither dead nor alive. That's why they are sometimes called the living dead – but there is a way to cure them!

ZOMBIE SLAVES

The idea of a zombie comes from voodoo – a religion that still has many followers today in Haiti and other Caribbean countries. Zombies aren't dead, but they aren't really alive either! Instead, they exist in a strange, trance-like state with no will of their own. According to Caribbean folklore, zombies were once used as cheap labour. They require very little food and will do anything their master tells them to do.

COURTING TROUBLE

You might think that zombies are just another made-up horror story. If so, think again! Less than 200 years ago, the government of Haiti took the problem of zombies so seriously that it passed a law making it an offence to turn someone into a zombie.

Index

Quiz answers

- **Page 3** a, they pushed a wooden spike into his eye while he was asleep; b, he unravelled some wool, leaving a trail behind him; a, it could revive the dead.
- **Page 4** b, refused to make him a girlfriend; c, *Treasure Island*; c, he had built the gallows on which he was executed.
- **Page 7** b, yeti; a, Alama; b, a prehistoric creature that lived in water.
- **Page 8** c, Wales; b, Python; a, England.
- **Page 11** b, Romania; c; mice; a, Central and South America.
- **Page 12** c, 75 or more; a, lycanthrope; c, 1680.
- **Page 15** c, Iblis; b, a marsupial; c, Lucifer.
- **Page 16** a, a deadly bacteria sealed in the tomb; a, 18; c, a dried-out dead body.
- **Page 18** c, William Shakespeare; b, a coven; a, a hex.

- **Page 21** c, a big bonfire to scare away evil spirits; a, a Roman festival held on Hallowe'en in honour of the dead; a, Snap Apple Night.
- **Page 22** b, Bela Lugosi; c, Wednesday; a, William Henry Pratt.
- **Page 25** a, Anne Boleyn; a, A Christmas Carol; b, appearing while people are having a bath.
- **Page 26** c, the ship's captain made a bet with the devil and lost; a, sea lion or sea cow; b, 3.
- **Page 29** b, Samuel Johnson; a, Roman times; b, detecting slight vibrations or movements.
- **Page 30** a, a witch doctor; a, Christian and African beliefs; a, Houngan.

Acknowledgements

Copyright © 2006 **ticktock** Entertainment Ltd. First published in Great Britain by ticktock Media Ltd.,
Unit 2, Orchard Business Centre, North Farm Road, Tunbridge Wells, Kent TN2 3XF, Great Britain.
All rights reserved. No part of this publication may be reproduced, stored in a retrieval system, or transmitted in any form or by any means electronic, mechanical, photocopying, recording or otherwise, without prior written permission of the copyright owner.
A CIP catalogue record for this book is available from the British Library.
ISBN 1 86007 959 8 Printed in China.
Picture Credits: t = top, b = bottom, c = centre, l = left, r=right, OFC = outside front cover, OBC = outside back cover, IFC = inside front cover
Ann Ronan @ Image select; 10/11, 16b. AKG Photo; 2/3, 2b, 4/5b, 8/9,10b, 12b, 18/19, 23b. Fortean Picture Library; IFC, 6/7, 6b, 12/13t, 25, 25/26, 28. Image Select; 20/21t,
20/21. PIX; 27. Planet Earth Pictures; 14/15. Rex Picture; 8b. Telegraph Colour Library; 26. The Kobal Collection; OFC (main pic), 4/5t, 14t, 16/17, 19b, 22/23, 29, 30/31, 31.